Changing sounds

A brief history

TODAY... 1890s American physicist Wallace Sabine is the first person to study how sound moves in a room. He also begins the study of soundproofing... 1880s The rise of the motor car quickly results in the design of silencers... 1809 Ernst Chladni, in Germany, is the first to sprinkle sand onto a metal sheet and then see patterns appear as the metal sheet is vibrated. He also makes the first measurement of the speed of sound in iron... 1660 Robert Hooke, in England, is the first person to produce a sound by making a string vibrate a known number of times a second using a spinning, toothed wheel... 1660 Robert Boyle, in England, and Athanasius Kircher in 1650 in Rome, put a bell in a jar and pump out all of the air. The bell can no longer be heard, showing that sound needs air to travel through... 1600 Galileo Galilei, in Italy, investigates sound and vibrations, founding the science of the study of sound... 350BC Greek scientist Aristotle suggests that a sound wave moves by disturbing the air... 500BC Greek mathematician Pythagoras experiments with vibrating strings to find which kinds of vibrations produce pleasing sounds... 1350BC Trumpets are in use in Egypt... 1600BC Natural ram and other animal horns are used as musical instruments... 2700BC Reeds are used to make sounds in Egypt... 4000BC Flutes and harps are being used in the Middle East... 25,000BC Simple wind and percussion instruments (such as sticks banged together) are recorded on cave paintings in France...

For more information visit www.curriculumvisions.com

Word list

These are some science words that you should look out for as you go through the book. They are shown using CAPITAL letters.

AMPLIFY
To make bigger. When sound is amplified it gets louder.

DAMPING
To make less noisy. A damper, often in the form of a pad placed on the vibrating object, is used to reduce vibrations.

DECIBEL
A measurement of the loudness of a sound.

ECHO
The sound that rebounds from hard surfaces and is heard, slightly changed, a little after the direct sound.

ENERGY
The ability to make something happen.

MUFFLE
To cover or wrap up something in order to reduce the loudness of the sound it is producing.

NOISE
An unwanted or loud sound. Most noises are made of a mixture of sounds, rather than the simple sounds, like musical notes, which we think are pleasant.

NOTE
A vibration that matches a place on a musical scale.

OCTAVE
A range of eight notes, for example from middle C to the next C above or below it.

PITCH
A word used in music to describe the vibrations that make a sound. The faster a vibration is, the higher the pitch. For example, a treble sound is high-pitched and a bass sound is low-pitched.

POWER
The amount of energy each second.

REED
A small, flexible piece of material that vibrates rapidly when air is blown across it.

REFLECT
To bounce from a surface. Sound reflects in much the same way as light.

RESONANCE
A vibration that builds on itself, causing the vibration to build up to be much larger than usual.

SOUND
Vibrations that can be heard. Sound travels through a material whether you can see through it or not; it cannot travel through space.

SOUNDPROOFING
The use of materials to cut out sounds. Sound will not travel through a vacuum and so a vacuum is very effective in soundproofing.

SOUND WAVE
The pattern of vibrations that travels away from the source of a sound and spreads out, much like ripples in a pond.

TENSION
Stretching tightly. Strings, when they are tight, are under tension.

TUNE, TUNING
To adjust the vibrations of, for example, a string on a piano, until the vibrations match those made by a tuning fork.

VACUUM
A place where there is no air.

VIBRATION
The rapid movement of an object, such as a drum skin. The result often produces a sound.

2

Contents

Weblink: www.curriculumvisions.com

Feeling and seeing sounds

A SOUND is a very quick VIBRATION. We can hear and feel many vibrations.

You can hear lots of sounds: voices, the sound of breaking glass, and musical instruments such as cymbals being clashed or a drum being struck. But how does sound reach our ears?

Feeling sound

You can feel sound being made if you place your finger gently onto the surface of a loudspeaker while it is working (Picture 1). You will feel the loudspeaker moving back and forth very quickly. This kind of movement is called a vibration.

If you tap an instrument such as a drum or tambourine and gently feel the skin, you can also feel the vibrations. You can even pluck the string of a guitar or violin and feel the string moving up and down – it is also vibrating.

Finally, if you place a finger gently on the lower part of your throat and sing a deep note, you can then feel your throat vibrating too. So now we know that where there is a vibration, there is a sound.

Seeing vibrations

Vibrations can be seen, as well as felt and heard, by using a tuning fork and a piece of cling film. The cling film needs to be tightly stretched over a jar and then covered in very fine grains of sand or rice (Picture 2).

When the tuning fork is struck and placed so that it touches the cling film very lightly, the vibrations will make the sand or rice on the film jump up and down.

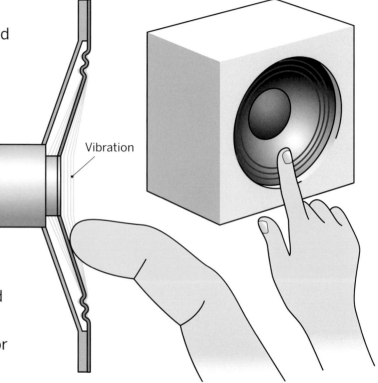

Vibration

▲ **(Picture 1) You can feel sound by gently touching a loudspeaker while sound is coming from it.**

▼▶ **(Picture 2) Vibrations can be seen by placing a vibrating tuning fork on a tightly stretched skin covered in sand.**

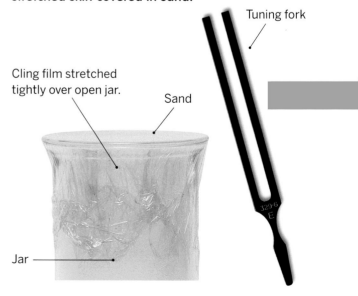

Cling film stretched tightly over open jar.

Sand

Tuning fork

Jar

4

Vibrations through air

You can see vibrations pass through the air by using a candle, a cardboard tube and some thin plastic sheet (Picture 3). Stretch the plastic tightly over both ends of the tube and make a small hole in the centre of one piece of plastic.

When the far side of the tube is tapped sharply, the air inside the tube is squashed slightly. As the air is forced out of the tube through the small hole, the **ENERGY** in the squashed air is concentrated. As a result, a sharp jet of air comes out of the hole and makes the flame wobble!

Q How can we see that a tuning fork vibrates when it makes a sound?

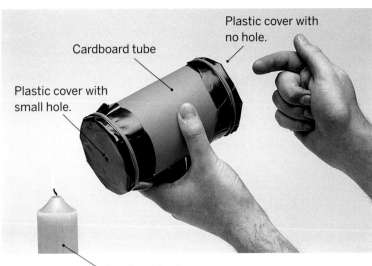

Plastic cover with no hole.

Cardboard tube

Plastic cover with small hole.

Candle with a long, thin flame.

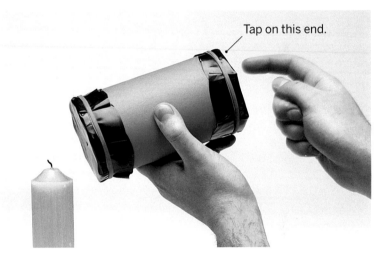

Tap on this end.

▲ (Picture 3) This is one way to 'see' SOUND WAVES. The plastic on the far end of the tube is struck sharply and the air waves are forced out of a small hole in the other end of the tube. The waves are powerful enough to make a candle flame move.

Summary

- Sounds are movements of the air that you can hear.
- Sound waves are made by a movement called a vibration.
- Vibrations cause air to move.

Weblink: www.curriculumvisions.com

How sounds travel

Sounds travel out from their sources and pass through materials such as air and wood.

Whenever something pushes against the air it squashes, or compresses, the air a little. The bunched-up air pushes against the air next to it, causing it to bunch up in turn.

▼ **(Picture 1) To help see how sound waves move through a material, you can use a coil of wire like a slinky. When you quickly tap one end, a wave of tightly packed coils moves along the slinky.**

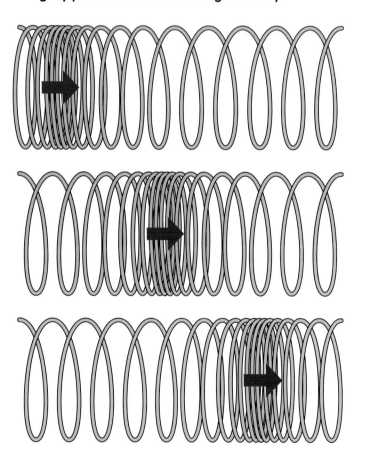

▶ **(Picture 2) When you pluck a guitar string, it moves up and down very rapidly. An elastic band does the same thing. This pushes and pulls against the air around it and sends out a sound.**

Imagining sound moving

Think of moving sound as like a row of people standing side by side. A person at one end of the row gently leans against their neighbour before standing upright again. The neighbour then does the same, and so on. Although each person has only moved a little in order to lean against their neighbour, the leaning moves right along the line. A 'slinky' shows this, too (Picture 1).

Notice that the coils in the slinky just rock to and fro. Exactly the same thing happens in air. The air doesn't move much, it just rocks to and fro as the region of squashing, or compression, passes through it.

In the same way, the push of a guitar string or elastic band against the air causes a band of squashed air to move from the string or band and through the air until it eventually reaches our ears and is heard as a sound (Picture 2).

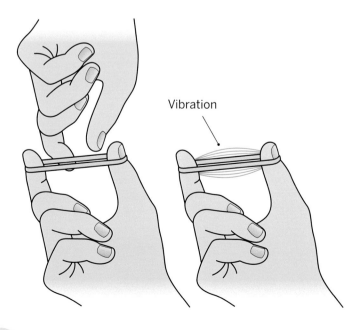

Vibration

Weblink: www.curriculumvisions.com

Sounds reach our ears

We call the vibrations that we can hear a **SOUND WAVE** and we show it on diagrams using curved lines (Picture 3) or a wavy line (Picture 4).

Sound is different from light

Sound needs a material to travel through.

Sound can travel through air, water or a solid object such as wood or steel. This is why you can hear a sound sent along a 'string telephone' (Picture 4). However, whereas light can travel through space, sound cannot. In space, there is nothing for the vibrations to pass through.

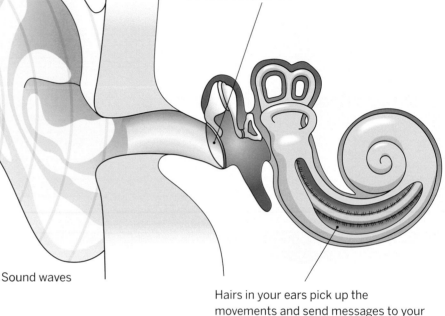

▼ (Picture 3) Sound waves travel into your ears where the movements are detected by your brain.

The movement of the air as the sound waves pass into your ear, moves your eardrum and the parts inside your ear.

Sound waves

Hairs in your ears pick up the movements and send messages to your brain which interprets them as sounds.

Summary
- **Sounds travel through materials.**
- **Sounds move by causing vibrations.**

Q How does sound reach our ears?

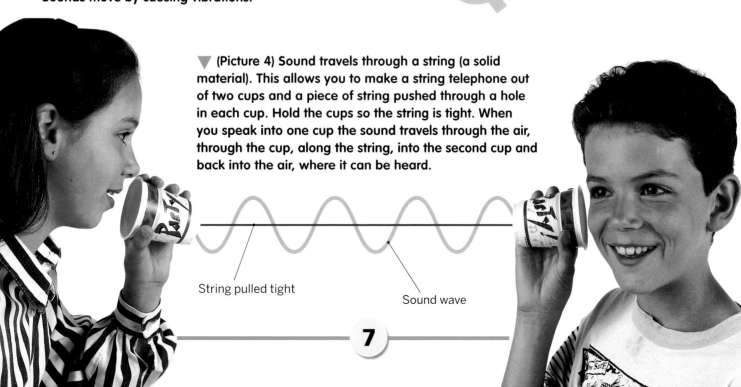

▼ (Picture 4) Sound travels through a string (a solid material). This allows you to make a string telephone out of two cups and a piece of string pushed through a hole in each cup. Hold the cups so the string is tight. When you speak into one cup the sound travels through the air, through the cup, along the string, into the second cup and back into the air, where it can be heard.

String pulled tight

Sound wave

How loud is a sound?

Sounds can vary in loudness depending on how much energy is in the waves.

Sound is a form of energy, just like light or heat. The more energy there is in a sound wave, the bigger the size of each vibration and the louder it sounds (Picture 1). The **POWER** of a sound is often measured in watts (W)

Ears and loudness

We are very sensitive to loudness, or sound level, so only small amounts of energy are needed to make a sound that we think is loud. A powerful hi-fi that would produce a deafening sound in a room might have a sound energy of 60 watts (W). But compared to a 60W light bulb or a 2,000W room heater this seems like a lot of sound for very little energy.

Making sounds louder and richer

The loudness of a sound depends on how much air vibrations can set in motion. If, for example, you hold a small electric motor in the air while it is running, it will be very quiet. If you then put the motor on a metal box, it will become much louder because the whole box also starts to vibrate and more air is set in motion. In this way a small sound has been made louder, or **AMPLIFIED**.

In the case of a motor, we usually want it to be as quiet as possible, but in some cases it is important to make sounds louder.

A loudspeaker held in the air, for example, is quiet and sounds very 'tinny' compared to the same loudspeaker in a cabinet (Picture 2).

The cabinet acts as a sound box, making the sound louder and richer. This effect is called **RESONANCE**. Many musical instruments, for example, violins, have cases which act as sound boxes (Picture 3).

Decibels

People measure sound loudness by a unit called a **DECIBEL** (dB).

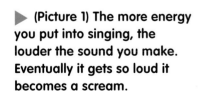

▶ **(Picture 1)** The more energy you put into singing, the louder the sound you make. Eventually it gets so loud it becomes a scream.

8

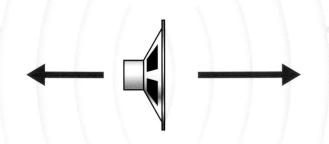

Zero decibels is the faintest sound we can hear, and 130dB is a sound so loud that it causes pain. Sound above 120dB is dangerous.

A television in a room may give out 30dB, while street traffic may be 70dB. People standing near to loudspeakers in concerts may get over 120dB. This is enough to make them temporarily deaf and may cause hearing damage.

Road drills and other machinery can also produce loud sounds, which is why people using them wear protective ear defenders (Picture 4) or use earplugs.

Q Why do loudspeakers and many musical instruments have 'sound boxes'?

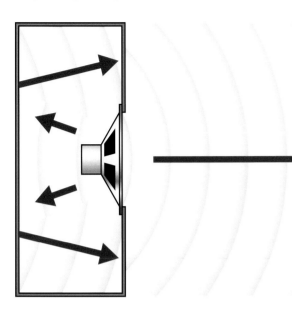

▲ (Picture 2) A loudspeaker sends out waves in front and behind. The cone of the speaker cannot vibrate well enough on its own, so the sound is quiet and 'tinny'. If the speaker is placed in a box, the box also vibrates. Because the box is bigger, the sound is louder and the box is better able to send out low notes. The sounds behind the loudspeaker bounce around inside the box and, if the design of the cabinet is right, they can add even more to the sound.

▶ (Picture 4) Ear defenders reduce sound.

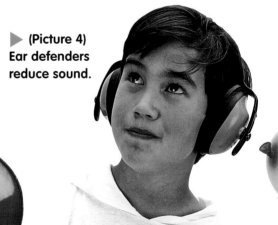

▶ (Picture 3) The body of a double bass is its sound box. Notice that the body has openings. These allow sound to get in and out of the sound box.

Summary

• A sound can be made louder by using a sound box.

• Sound is a form of energy. The more energy you put in, the louder the sound.

• Very loud sounds can be dangerous to your health.

Weblink: www.science-at-school.com

Sounds spread out

Sounds spread quite slowly in all directions, so the farther we are from a sound, the longer it takes to reach us and the quieter it seems.

To understand how sounds spread out, imagine throwing a pebble in a pond. It sends out ripples that make ever larger circles (Picture 1). You can imagine the ripples as sound waves. The ripples are highest near where the pebble was dropped, but as they spread out they become lower. It is the same with sound: the more the sound spreads out, the smaller the size of the vibration and the quieter it gets.

We can make a diagram to show this (Picture 2). The sound is loudest near the loudspeaker, where the sound is made. This is because the energy is still very concentrated. But as the waves spread out, the sound gets less concentrated. Eventually, the vibrations will be so small that the ear cannot detect it.

▲ **(Picture 1) Sound spreads out from a source just like ripples on a pond.**

How fast does sound spread out?

It takes several seconds for the sound caused by a flash of lightning to reach us as a clap of thunder. From this we can tell that sound moves much more slowly than light.

The speed at which sound travels depends on what it is travelling through. In air, it travels at about 330 metres per second, but it moves faster in water – nearly 1,500 metres per second, and faster still in steel – a whopping 5,000 metres per second.

Find the speed of sound

You can use clapping to work out the speed of sound. Simply stand 100 metres away from a tall wall and clap (Picture 3).

Change the rate of clapping until the sound bounced back from each clap matches your next clap. The sound has now travelled 200m between claps. Get someone to measure how many seconds it takes for you to make 10 claps at this rate. Divide this time by ten to find the time between each clap. The speed of sound is 200 divided by the time between claps. Check your answer against the value for the speed of sound given on this page.

Why does a sound appear quieter as we move away from it?

10

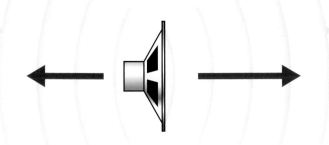

Zero decibels is the faintest sound we can hear, and 130dB is a sound so loud that it causes pain. Sound above 120dB is dangerous.

A television in a room may give out 30dB, while street traffic may be 70dB. People standing near to loudspeakers in concerts may get over 120dB. This is enough to make them temporarily deaf and may cause hearing damage.

Road drills and other machinery can also produce loud sounds, which is why people using them wear protective ear defenders (Picture 4) or use earplugs.

Q Why do loudspeakers and many musical instruments have 'sound boxes'?

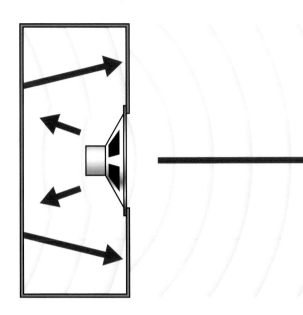

▲ (Picture 2) A loudspeaker sends out waves in front and behind. The cone of the speaker cannot vibrate well enough on its own, so the sound is quiet and 'tinny'. If the speaker is placed in a box, the box also vibrates. Because the box is bigger, the sound is louder and the box is better able to send out low notes. The sounds behind the loudspeaker bounce around inside the box and, if the design of the cabinet is right, they can add even more to the sound.

▶ (Picture 4) Ear defenders reduce sound.

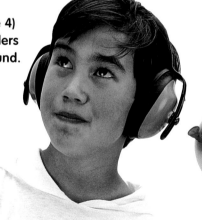

▶ (Picture 3) The body of a double bass is its sound box. Notice that the body has openings. These allow sound to get in and out of the sound box.

Summary

- A sound can be made louder by using a sound box.
- Sound is a form of energy. The more energy you put in, the louder the sound.
- Very loud sounds can be dangerous to your health.

9

Sounds spread out

Sounds spread quite slowly in all directions, so the farther we are from a sound, the longer it takes to reach us and the quieter it seems.

To understand how sounds spread out, imagine throwing a pebble in a pond. It sends out ripples that make ever larger circles (Picture 1). You can imagine the ripples as sound waves. The ripples are highest near where the pebble was dropped, but as they spread out they become lower. It is the same with sound: the more the sound spreads out, the smaller the size of the vibration and the quieter it gets.

We can make a diagram to show this (Picture 2). The sound is loudest near the loudspeaker, where the sound is made. This is because the energy is still very concentrated. But as the waves spread out, the sound gets less concentrated. Eventually, the vibrations will be so small that the ear cannot detect it.

How fast does sound spread out?

It takes several seconds for the sound caused by a flash of lightning to reach us as a clap of thunder. From this we can tell that sound moves much more slowly than light.

▲ (Picture 1) Sound spreads out from a source just like ripples on a pond.

The speed at which sound travels depends on what it is travelling through. In air, it travels at about 330 metres per second, but it moves faster in water – nearly 1,500 metres per second, and faster still in steel – a whopping 5,000 metres per second.

Find the speed of sound

You can use clapping to work out the speed of sound. Simply stand 100 metres away from a tall wall and clap (Picture 3).

Change the rate of clapping until the sound bounced back from each clap matches your next clap. The sound has now travelled 200m between claps. Get someone to measure how many seconds it takes for you to make 10 claps at this rate. Divide this time by ten to find the time between each clap. The speed of sound is 200 divided by the time between claps. Check your answer against the value for the speed of sound given on this page.

Why does a sound appear quieter as we move away from it?

Weblink: www.curriculumvisions.com

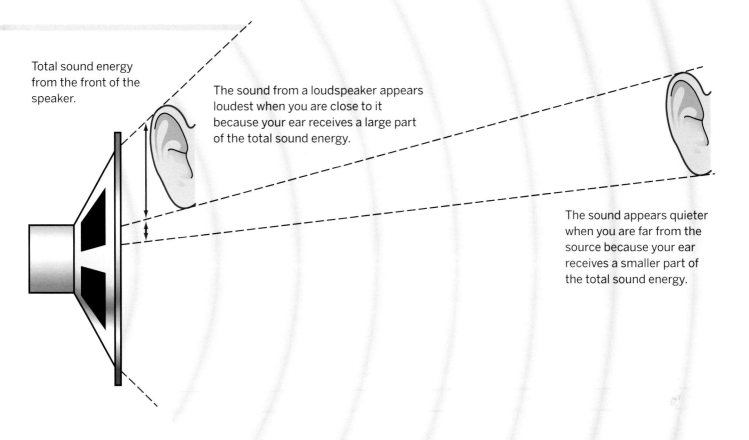

Total sound energy from the front of the speaker.

The sound from a loudspeaker appears loudest when you are close to it because your ear receives a large part of the total sound energy.

The sound appears quieter when you are far from the source because your ear receives a smaller part of the total sound energy.

▲ (Picture 2) Sound spreads out from a source such as a loudspeaker. The closer you are to the source, the more of the sound energy given out by the speaker reaches your ears and the louder it sounds.

▼ (Picture 3) The time it takes for a clap to bounce from a wall and back to your ears allows you to find the speed of sound.

Summary

• Because sounds spread out from a source, the energy of the sound also spreads out, so sounds get fainter the further away from them you are.

• Sound travels more slowly than light.

• Sound travels fastest in solids, less quickly in liquids, and slowest of all in air.

Echoes and reflections

Sound will bounce, or REFLECT, from hard surfaces. Sound reflections are called ECHOES.

Sound waves and light waves have many things in common. If you shine a light at a mirror, it will bounce, or be reflected back. If a sound hits a hard, flat surface, it too will bounce from that surface.

Reflected sound

If a sound hits a hard wall at an angle, it will bounce off at the same angle as it arrived (Picture 1) with little loss of loudness.

▲ **(Picture 1) When a sound hits a flat, hard surface, it bounces off at the same angle as it arrived. The reflected sound is only slightly quieter.**

If the surface is rough, the sound will bounce off in all directions (Picture 2), and anyone listening to the reflected sounds will hear only a quiet, **MUFFLED** sound. We shall see how important this is later.

Echo

It takes longer for a sound to be heard which has travelled to a hard surface and then bounced back to your ear, than when it travels directly in a straight line. This is because the reflected sound has further to go.

In an ordinary living room, this difference is tiny, so direct and reflected sound reach your ears at more or less the same time. But if the room is large, such as a hall, then it takes so long for the sound to bounce back that the bounced sound reaches your ears well after the direct sound. As a result, you hear what seems like two separate sounds. The sounds that arrive later are called echoes (Picture 3).

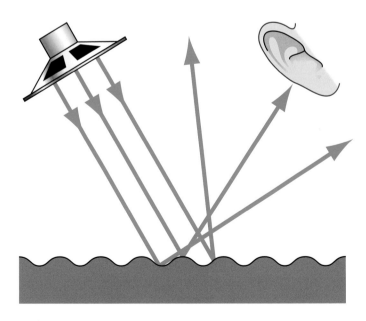

▲ **(Picture 2) When a sound hits a rough surface, the sound is scattered and the reflected sound is much fuzzier and quieter than the arriving sound.**

Weblink: www.curriculumvisions.com

▶ (Picture 3) In a hall with hard surfaces, sound is bounced from the walls and ceilings and does not arrive directly. The bounced sounds have further to travel, so they arrive later than the direct sound. This produces echoes.

Echo

Sound coming directly from a musician.

Spaces that echo

You may have wondered why caves, tunnels and some buildings echo more than other spaces (Picture 4). The answer is in their shape. Sound can be focused just like light. In a space with curved walls, almost all the sound is reflected back down towards the person who made the sound, producing extremely strong echoes (Picture 5).

▼ (Picture 4) This cathedral is the sort of large building that causes echoes. The many shapes of the walls and roof mean that the sound will bounce back and echo in a very complicated way.

▼ (Picture 5) Echoes in a tunnel or cave.

Summary
• Sound waves bounce from hard surfaces.
• Echoes are formed if sound bounces in large halls.

Q

Why are some places echoey?

Weblink: www.curriculumvisions.com

Damping sounds

Sounds are made quieter by stopping things from vibrating.

▲ **(Picture 2) Holding your finger firmly on the loudspeaker will make the sound coming from it quieter.**

Some materials make an unpleasantly loud sound if they are allowed to vibrate freely. To make these sounds quieter we need to make the vibrations smaller. This is called **DAMPING**. Examples of dampers include the rubber feet fitted to washing machines (Picture 1) and fish tank pumps.

Dampers can simply *flatten* a sound, or make it quieter (Picture 2). They can also be used to *change* a sound, as is the case with pianos, in which felt dampers are used to reduce the loudness of the piano (see page 22).

▲ **(Picture 1) The vibrations from a washing machine sitting on a floor could become unbearable. Rubber feet help damp the vibrations.**

Investigate damping

Clamp a long ruler or other springy material to the edge of a table (Picture 3). Now push down the free end and let it go. The ruler will twang, or vibrate.

Write down the approximate size of the vibration and time how long it takes to stop.

Loop a small elastic band around the ruler and pull upwards gently, then press down on the end of the ruler (Picture 4). Now twang the ruler again and see how long it takes for the vibrations to die down. Listen for the change in sound loudness.

▼ **(Picture 3) You can measure the size of the vibration by marking it with a pencil like this.**

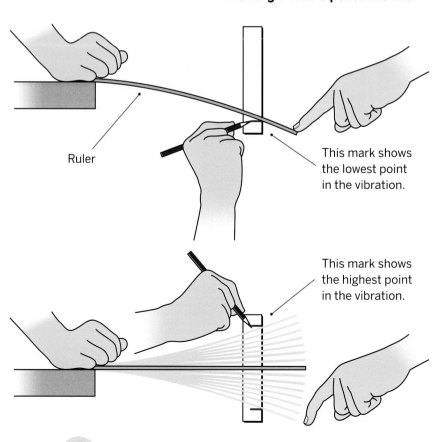

Ruler

This mark shows the lowest point in the vibration.

This mark shows the highest point in the vibration.

14

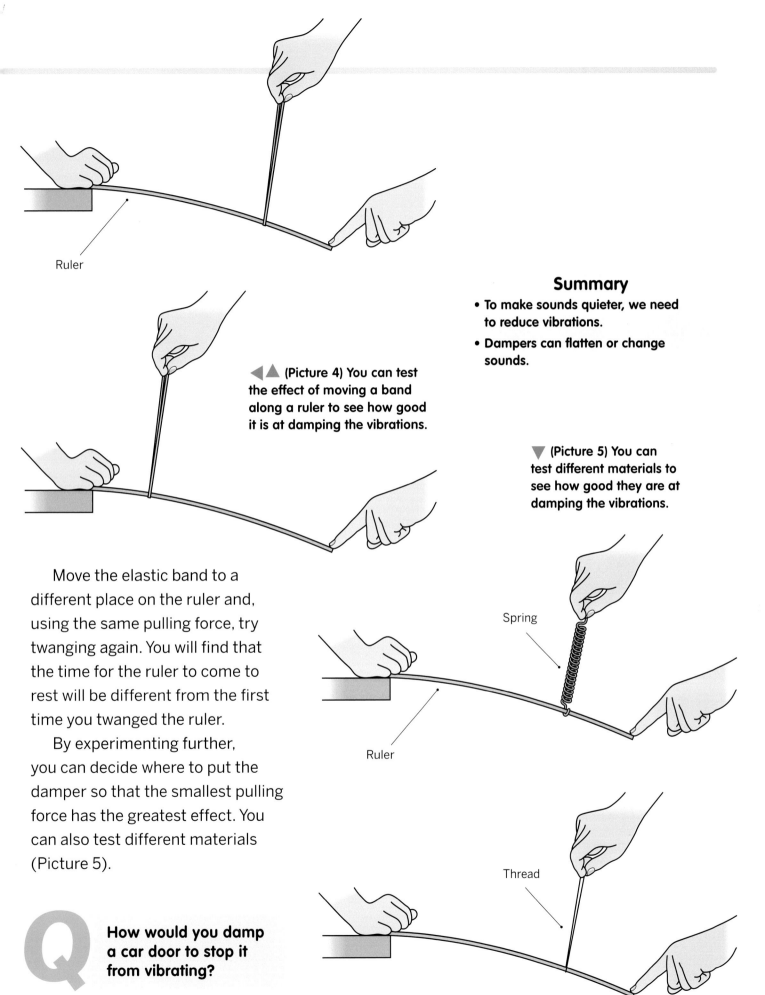

Ruler

(Picture 4) You can test the effect of moving a band along a ruler to see how good it is at damping the vibrations.

Summary
- To make sounds quieter, we need to reduce vibrations.
- Dampers can flatten or change sounds.

(Picture 5) You can test different materials to see how good they are at damping the vibrations.

Move the elastic band to a different place on the ruler and, using the same pulling force, try twanging again. You will find that the time for the ruler to come to rest will be different from the first time you twanged the ruler.

By experimenting further, you can decide where to put the damper so that the smallest pulling force has the greatest effect. You can also test different materials (Picture 5).

Spring

Ruler

Thread

Q How would you damp a car door to stop it from vibrating?

15

Muffling sound

You can MUFFLE, or reduce, sound by using soft materials.

So far in this book we have seen that sound needs a material to move in, and that it cannot travel through empty space. It can be bounced easily off hard, smooth surfaces, but not rough ones; it can travel through air, water and solids; it can be made louder by using a hollow box or sounding board. We need to know all of these things because **SOUNDPROOFING** is about trying to cut down unwanted sounds, or **NOISE**.

Double glazing

There is no air in space. This is called a **VACUUM**. Sound cannot travel through a vacuum.

Even taking out some air will help soundproofing because there is less air for sound to travel through. The most common example of this is double glazing (Picture 1). In double glazing, two sheets of glass are sealed together, leaving just a small gap between them. Some air is then removed from the gap, making double-glazed windows good at keeping out noise.

Materials that soak up vibrations

The best material to soak up sounds is soft, spongy or porous – something that has a rough surface with lots of holes in. The sound goes into the holes, bounces around inside and never comes out. Curtains, carpets and other fabrics in a room are all

Most of the air between the sheets of glass is taken out to make double glazing.

▲ **(Picture 1) Double glazing is a good muffler of sound.**

▼ **(Picture 2) Curtains are made of many fibres. They muffle sounds well.**

good soundproofing, or muffling, materials (Picture 2). This is why a room that is empty echoes, but a room full of furniture, carpet and curtains does not.

Soft plastic foam works the same way.

Stopping sound from travelling

Sound travels much faster, and for longer distances, through solids than through the air. This means that if you make a noise in one room, it will travel through the solid walls, ceilings and floors to rooms quite a long way away.

When buildings are made, strips of rubber or other soundproofing materials are often laid between walls, ceiling and floor, to stop sound travelling easily through the building.

Car silencers

If you heard a car without a silencer, it would be painfully noisy and sound like a cannon being fired very fast. To muffle the sound, a car is fitted with a device called a silencer (Picture 3).

Some silencers are filled with wadding made of fine fibres. The sound coming from the engine makes all of these fibres vibrate. This changes sound energy to heat energy.

In other silencers the sound is also bounced between the two ends of the silencer. The length of the silencer is arranged so that when the bounced sounds meet they mostly cancel each other out. This is exactly the opposite of what happens in a musical instrument (page 19), where the aim is to make the sound louder.

Summary

- **Muffling aims to stop sound from travelling.**
- **Soundproofing materials are usually soft or loose, and have many holes or gaps in them.**
- **Double glazing can also reduce noise.**

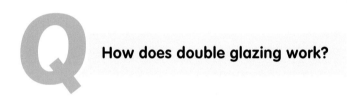

Q **How does double glazing work?**

Sound (shown by the curved pink lines) bounces back and forth using up energy and getting quieter.

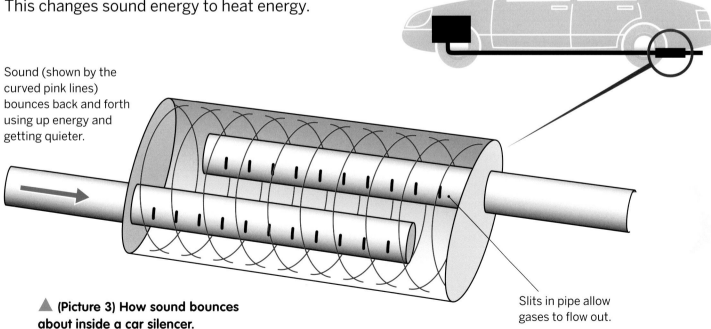

Slits in pipe allow gases to flow out.

▲ **(Picture 3) How sound bounces about inside a car silencer.**

Making a musical sound

A musical sound is made by a simple, regular vibration.

To most of us a musical instrument makes a pleasant sound. This is different from the unpleasant sounds that we call noise.

Music is made of regular vibrations

Our ears can pick up many kinds of sound, even complicated ones. But if the sound is very complicated, our brain often thinks of it as noise.

Most musical instruments produce fairly pure sounds called **NOTES**. A pure sound is produced, for example, when a guitar string is plucked and the string vibrates up and down in a simple, regular way.

A tuning fork

A tuning fork (Picture 1) produces just a single, pure musical sound. When one of the prongs is tapped on a hard surface, both prongs vibrate in a simple way to give a pure note.

▲ **(Picture 1) A tuning fork vibrates to produce a single, pure sound.**

Simple ways of making notes

Simple musical instruments can be made using the principle of the tuning fork.

For example, a musical instrument capable of playing eight notes (an **OCTAVE**) can be made from eight bottles (Picture 2). Each bottle is filled with a different amount of water. This changes the length of the air space in each bottle and affects the vibrations and the **PITCH** (highness or lowness) of the note.

▼ **(Picture 2) A set of bottles that can play a scale covering one octave.**

18

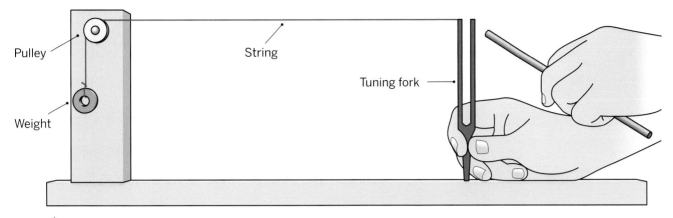

▲ (Picture 3) How a tuning fork vibrates to produce a single, pure sound.

Pulley

String

Tuning fork

Weight

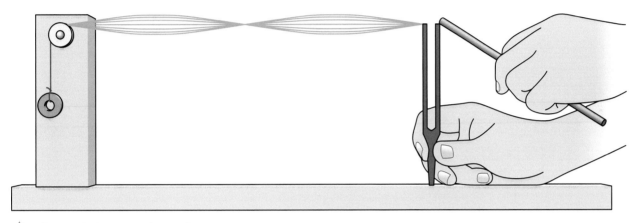

▲ (Picture 4) A resonating string.

Each bottle is tapped with a drumstick or pen. By changing the amount of water in each bottle, the notes can be adjusted to match the notes on a piano. Once you have done this, the bottles will each produce a simple note and together they make a scale.

Musical string

To see how the vibrations work in a musical instrument, you can attach a thin length of string to a tuning fork and a weight (Picture 3). Tap the tuning fork and watch the string vibrate. There will be several places with no vibrations and other places where the string vibrates strongly. Waves are travelling back and forth along the string in time with the vibrations of the tuning fork, but the to and fro movements are in step and so the wave appears to be standing still (Picture 4). This is called **RESONATING** and it is the pattern of waves that occurs inside every musical instrument.

By changing the distance between fork and pulley, you can see and hear the sound for different patterns of vibration.

 How can you change the note a string plays?

Summary
- A musical sound is a regular vibration.
- A tuning fork is a single, pure note.
- You can change the note of a musical instrument by changing the length of the part that vibrates.

Weblink: www.curriculumvisions.com

Wind instruments

Wind instruments work by setting a column of air vibrating.

When you blow over the end of a bottle, you push steady pulses of air down the bottle (Picture 1). The air from each pulse then bounces back up.

If the rate at which you send pulses is just right, the air resonates.

You can alter the note by changing the length of the space in the bottle, for example, by adding water or choosing a longer or shorter bottle.

Short pipe length will resonate to give a high pitch.

Long pipe length will resonate to give a low pitch.

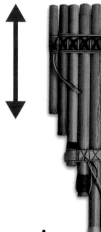

How wind instruments work

All wind instruments make sounds in the same way as the bottle (Picture 2).

A recorder is a simple wind instrument (Picture 3). When you blow into the mouthpiece, its design sends a stream of air pulsing out over the sharp edge of the mouthpiece and we hear a note.

The recorder body has holes drilled in it. As these are opened and closed, using the fingers, they change the length of the recorder and change the note.

◀ **(Picture 1) As you blow across the top of a bottle, you can set up vibrations that bounce around inside the bottle and resonate.**

▶ **(Picture 2) With pan pipes, the different length tubes each produce a different pitch.**

A flute is like a recorder turned on its side. In this case, you blow over the mouthpiece hole just as you did over the top of the bottle.

Instruments such as the oboe, clarinet and saxophone (Picture 4) have a **REED** in the mouthpiece. The reed vibrates when air is blown over it and this sets the air in the instrument vibrating.

Vibrating reed

Q Why does closing the holes in a recorder change the note it makes?

▲▶ (Picture 4) The saxophone is a reed instrument. The vibrating reed produces the sound that is then adjusted using a complex arrangement of holes.

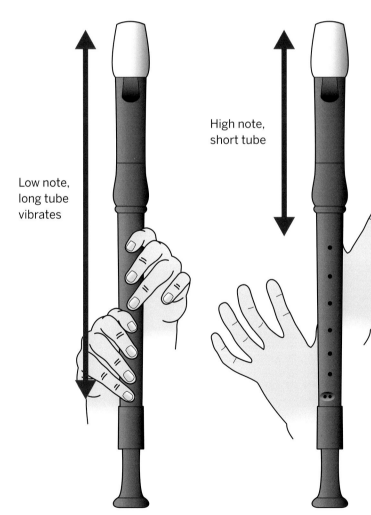

High note, short tube

Low note, long tube vibrates

▲ (Picture 3) With a recorder, you alter the length of the tube by closing your fingers over the holes.

Summary

- Wind instruments make a sound when a column of air inside them vibrates.
- The length of vibrating air is altered by covering holes, using fingers or keys.
- In some wind instruments, a reed is used to set up vibrations.

String instruments

String instruments work by making a string vibrate.

There are several ways in which a string can be made to vibrate. The string can be struck (as in a piano), plucked (as in a guitar) or a bow can be scraped across it (as in a violin).

▼ **(Pictures 1 and 2) A piano has many strings, all held in a frame. When you press a key on the keyboard, levers make a hammer tap the string quickly.**

The piano is actually 88 separate musical instruments all put together in a single frame. You need a separate hammer – and therefore a separate key – for each note.

Fixed length strings

Instruments like the piano have strings stretched over a strong metal frame. The hammer strikes the string and causes it to vibrate at the note it has been **TUNED** to (Pictures 1 and 2).

4 The vibration of the string makes the sound. Longer strings make deeper sounds and shorter strings make higher sounds.

3 The hammer strikes the string and causes a vibration.

5 A damper stops the string vibrating as the key is released.

2 The lever attached to the key lifts the jack, which flicks the hammer.

1 Key is pressed down.

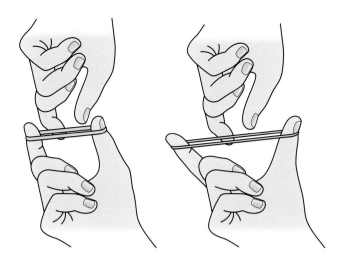

▲ (Picture 3) Changing the pitch of an elastic band by increasing the tension.

Changing the string length

Instruments where the fingers touch the strings have a much smaller number of strings. In this case, the individual notes are produced by placing a finger on the string as it crosses the fingerboard. To produce a higher note, the string is shortened by pressing on it. The longer, or thicker, strings produce the lower notes.

In string instruments the strings are stretched and held tight. To see the effect of changing the tightness, or **TENSION**, in the string, hook an elastic band over two fingers and pull the band taut. Now pluck it (Picture 3). Pull harder and pluck again. The band is now under greater tension and the pitch will be higher.

Violin

In a violin, there is a set of four strings (Picture 4). They are tightened, and tuned, by the pegs at the end of the fingerboard.

The strings are stretched over a small wooden frame called a bridge. Below the bridge, and inside the violin, is a post that connects the front and back of the case.

When the violin bow scrapes across the strings, the juddering motion causes the string to vibrate. The vibration of the strings goes through the bridge and into the body of the violin.

The body of the violin acts as a sound box, causing the sound to bounce back and forth (resonate) inside the violin, making the sound louder and richer.

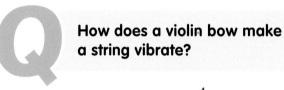

Q How does a violin bow make a string vibrate?

Fingerboard

▲ (Picture 4) In a violin, the bow pulls the strings sideways.

Summary

- **String instruments work through the vibration of a string.**
- **In some instruments, separate strings are used to make individual notes.**
- **In instruments such as guitars and violins, the notes are produced by changing the length of the strings using the fingers or a bow.**

Weblink: www.curriculumvisions.com

Index

Curriculum Visions

Science@School

Teacher's Guide

There is a Teacher's Guide to accompany this book, available only from the publisher.

There's much more online including videos

You will find multimedia resources covering this and ALL 37 QCA Key Stage 1 and 2 science units as well as history, geography, religion, MFL, maths, music, spelling and more at:

www.CurriculumVisions.com

(Subscription required)

A CVP Book
This second edition © Atlantic Europe Publishing 2011

First edition 2002. First reprint 2004.
Second reprint 2006.

The right of Brian Knapp to be identified as the author of this work has been asserted by him in accordance with the Copyright, Designs and Patents Act 1988.

All rights reserved. No part of this publication may be reproduced, stored in a retrieval system, or transmitted in any form or by any means, electronic, mechanical, photocopying, recording or otherwise, without prior permission of the copyright holder.

Author
Brian Knapp, BSc, PhD

Educational Consultant
Peter Riley, BSc, C Biol, MI Biol, PGCE

Art Director
Duncan McCrae, BSc

Senior Designer
Adele Humphries, BA, PGCE

Editor
Lisa Magloff, MA

Illustrations
David Woodroffe

Designed and produced by
Atlantic Europe Publishing

Printed in China by
WKT Company Ltd

Volume 5F *Changing sounds 2nd Edition*
– Curriculum Visions Science@School
A CIP record for this book is available from the British Library.

Paperback ISBN 978 1 86214 678 5

Picture credits
All photographs are from the Earthscape and ShutterStock collections.

This product is manufactured from sustainable managed forests. For every tree cut down at least one more is planted.